That Wolfdog Lifestyle

Published in Canada by Iceberg Publishing, Edmonton, Alberta

Library and Archives Canada Cataloguing in Publication

Title: That wolfdog lifestyle at Yamnuska Wolfdog Sanctuary / Georgina De Caigny, Jeannine Göhing, Alyx Harris, Jacqui Tam, Kenneth Tam, Peter Tam.
Names: De Caigny, Georgina, 1989- author. | Göhing, Jeannine, 1987- author. | Harris, Alyx, 1993- author. | Tam, Kenneth, 1984- author. | Tam, Jacqui, 1960- editor. | Tam, Peter, 1957- photographer.
Identifiers: Canadiana (print) 20200231383 | Canadiana (ebook) 20200231391 | ISBN 9781989815021 (hardcover) | ISBN 9781989815014 (softcover) | ISBN 9781989815007 (ebook)
Subjects: LCSH: Wolfdogs—Conservation—Alberta—Cochrane. | LCSH: Wolfdogs—Behavior. | LCSH: Animal rescue—Alberta—Cochrane. | LCSH: Wildlife refuges—Alberta—Cochrane. | LCSH: Yamnuska Wolfdog Sanctuary.
Classification: LCC QL737.C22 D43 2020 | DDC 599.77/2—dc23

Digital edition ISBN: 978-1-989815-00-7
Softcover ISBN: 978-1-989815-01-4
Hardcover ISBN: 978-1-989815-02-1

First published: May 2020

Text Contributors: Georgina De Caigny, Jeannine Göhing, Alyx Harris, Kenneth Tam, Jacqui Tam

Photography By: Georgina De Caigny, Jeannine Göhing, Jacqui Tam, Kenneth Tam, Peter Tam

Cover and Layout Design: Kenneth Tam

Iceberg Publishing
301-14032 23 Ave NW
Edmonton, AB Canada T6R 3L6
icebergpublishing.com

That Wolfdog Lifestyle

at Yamnuska Wolfdog Sanctuary

Georgina De Caigny Jeannine Göhing Alyx Harris
Jacqui Tam Kenneth Tam Peter Tam

Introduction

The story of Canada's first and only wolfdog sanctuary began when Georgina and Kuna met.

Being a seasoned dog owner, Georgina instantly fell in love with the smart, beautiful pup. She was only 19 years old when Kuna — a high content wolfdog — came home with her, and she had no idea what she had gotten herself into. Struggling with first-time wolfdog ownership, Georgina went through a massive reality check. No manner of experience with dogs prepares one for dealing with a high content wolfdog, and Kuna helped Georgina realize that high content wolfdogs are not suitable as regular pets.

By getting a lot of things wrong initially, Georgina learned many hard lessons. Among them was the fact that a person needs to adapt to a wolfdog — not the other way round. She had to make sacrifices and compromises, and live a lifestyle suitable for Kuna. She also had to re-educate herself as a pet owner, and learn what it means to responsibly care for a wolfdog.

Through all of this, Georgina also realized that, like herself, most people don't know what it takes to care for — and contain — a wolfdog. Rebuilding her life around Kuna inspired her to help more wolfdogs, as well as the people who find themselves in a similar situation to hers.

When she discovered that there were no wolfdog rescues in Canada, she turned away from a career in engineering and took matters into her own hands.

Georgina started the Yamnuska Wolfdog Sanctuary with Kuna in 2011 on a small property in Canmore, Alberta, Canada. Her mission was to create a safe haven for displaced wolfdogs and provide education on all things related to wolfdogs and wolves.

After four years of rapid growth, she moved the Sanctuary to a 160-acre plot just outside of Cochrane, Alberta — about 75 kilometers away — where she and her dedicated team of staff and volunteers now care for 25 permanent wolfdogs divided into 10 packs named for mountains in the Canadian Rockies, which stand tall nearby. Yamnuska — named for the mountain that guarded the original Sanctuary in Canmore — welcomes hundreds of visitors every week, and provides daily educational tours.

The Sanctuary provides wolfdogs with large natural enclosures including a diverse range of vegetation to ensure a healthy and stress-free environment. The team also provides the wolfdogs with enrichment items such as water tanks, toys, platforms, and even a tree house! Part of the Sanctuary's mission is the rescue of wolfdogs that have been neglected, abandoned, or otherwise displaced or mistreated, and providing these animals with the care they need to be rehabilitated and rehomed.

Georgina's passion and commitment, combined with the lessons she and Kuna learned together, have paved the way for dozens of rescues, and built the foundation for a facility unlike any other in Canada. The Yamnuska Wolfdog Sanctuary is a place for people to learn about wolfdogs, responsible wolfdog ownership, the challenges of being a wolfdog owner, and what a suitable wolfdog home looks like.

In this book, you will be introduced to the current resident wolfdogs, with stories that highlight quirks about their personalities and some 200 photos that are sure to delight. If you've been to the Sanctuary, you might recognize your favourite friends. If you haven't been there yet, you'll soon want to visit!

Never in a million years did Georgina imagine the impact the Yamnuska Wolfdog Sanctuary would have, or the passion and care that its growing community would share for each and every wolfdog. Enjoy this virtual visit with the wolfdog family, and they'll look forward to seeing you soon!

Yamnuska Pack

(the original)

Kuna, Zeus, Nova, Nikki & Ylva

Have to
get ready
for the
photo
book...
Ahhh.
Ready.

Kuna (high content & alpha female)

Together with her incredible human Georgina, Kuna helped launch Canada's first and only wolfdog sanctuary! She has an amazing ability to communicate exactly what she wants, whether it's another raw meat patty or some extra love and attention. She is very smart and independent, but can also be quite stubborn. Kuna was born in May 2009 at a private wolf facility in Saskatchewan. She founded the Yamnuska wolfdog family as an 11-week-old puppy after her previous owners felt she was too difficult to handle, and she moved in with Georgina.

Breakfast
with Kuna

ZEUS (high content & alpha male)

Often affectionately called Yamnuska's "grumpy old man," Zeus actually really loves receiving pets from those with whom he feels comfortable. He was the first rescued wolfdog to join Kuna at the Sanctuary, blazing a trail that many more followed! He was born in April 2010 and came to Yamnuska in June 2011 as a one-year old puppy after his owner was no longer able to provide the proper care and containment needed for him to be happy and safe. He's also Kuna's half-brother — can you tell?

I will now
stand for
my portrait
Behind me?
HEY!
Hmph.

Nova (high content)

As an arctic wolfdog, Nova is a real exception among Yamnuska's wolfdogs, thanks to his beautiful pure-white coat. He's also one of the most hard-wired wolfdogs at the Sanctuary, but can be very sweet and loving with the people he knows. He has a strong bond with his alpha male Zeus, often sharing generous licks and tail wags! He's also a real crowd-pleaser (goofball). Watch out for his impressive jumps and paw-waves, and his play sessions with his pack!

Nova the Goalie
(goalkeeper)
Incoming!
up!
up!
SLOW-MO!
one for the highlight reel!
Next round.
Let's go!

Nikki (low content)

When Yamnuska's staff first met Nikki in November 2012, she was completely feral — wild and untamed. Of all the wolfdogs at the Sanctuary, she has shown the most substantial transformation! Now, although still a bit timid, you can see her asking for belly rubs and butt scratches from visitors. Despite being low content, Nikki clearly loves her high content pack mates — she whines and howls when separated from them.

Hang on there's something on your face!
Almost got it...
Switch sides!
IT'S FINE.

Ylva (high content)

Being the youngest wolfdog of the Yamnuska pack, and in the Sanctuary, Ylva is a bit of a troublemaker. She truly loves playing with her pack — watch her tugging the tails of her pack mates, and their reactions — but she can also easily entertain herself. Ylva came to the Sanctuary as a four-month old puppy from an organization in British Columbia. She was immensely fearful and shy at first but has really come out of her shell!

Mischief with Ylva
What are you up to, kid?
Don't say 'nothing'.
Ever since you were a pup...
...You've been an adorable troublemaker!

NOTHING!
I'll be right back.
Great.
Hmm.
Does he notice me waiting?
I'll just let him know I'm here.
Zeus looks busy.
Owww my TAIL!
YLVA!!!...

Cascade Pack

Loki, Rocky & Rue (welcoming committee)

Everyone clean up!
They're making a book about us!
How's this?
I'm sure you look fine.
Added a bow.

Loki (low content)

Named for the Norse god of mischief, Loki certainly can live up to his name — he needs to be closely monitored in certain situations! He also really loves greeting visitors and can be seen wagging his tail and offering paw shakes to everyone he meets. He arrived at the Sanctuary from Edmonton Animal Control in 2014.

Choir Practice
with Loki

Rocky (low content)

At 16 years old, Rocky enjoys spending his days snoozing... but can turn into an energetic puppy whenever it's tour time and the treats appear! He's the most senior wolfdog at the Sanctuary, and sometimes he can be a bit impatient and pushy, but he's loved unconditionally all the same. Originally confiscated from a bad backyard breeder, Rocky enjoys his retirement at Yamnuska. Despite his age and senior moments, you'll see that he's a fairly easy-going guy!

Hey.
Hey,
c'mon.
only if they
have treats.
Lazy day
with
Rocky

Rue (upper mid content)

Rue joined the Sanctuary to do an important job: she's an ambassador animal and has truly excelled in that role! She's also a bit of a tomboy, and loves rough-housing with her pack mate Loki. She has a very goofy, fun-loving personality and is well known for her "Rue hugs" with the Sanctuary staff. Rue can be shy of new people but is undoubtedly one of the most affectionate wolfdogs at the Sanctuary. She was born in Missouri in 2015.

Treasure
hunting
with Rue

Rundle Pack

Lark & Nakita (together forever)

Hey we need to move around for the book photo.
We moved.

Lark (high content)

Lark has earned quite the reputation as a charmer, thanks to his handsome looks and playful personality. His longtime pack mate is Nakita — they came to the Sanctuary together in December 2014 from a wildlife facility in Washington.

Nakita (high content)

Nakita had a very different introduction to the world: she was born with a degenerative eye condition, making her interactions with her environment and humans quite unique. She adores her human caretakers and becomes extremely excited at the mere sound of them approaching. She loves giving lots of kisses and is well known for her incredible spring-like bouncing in the air! Nakita came to the Sanctuary in December 2014 with her mate Lark.

Lark's mission...
Sneak...
Search...
Spot...
YES. Found the perfect gift...

Later...
Hey you, got you something for the bath...
It's a stick from the dandelions!
Aww... it's PERFECT!!!

Castle Pack

Horton & Kasha

Horton, hurry! Come and see this!
I'm here! What's happening?
They're going to photograph us for a book!
Oh. Uh. Do I have time to clean up?

Horton (low content)

Horton is uniquely handsome! Being mainly Irish Wolfhound, he's one of the most distinctive looking wolfdogs in the Yamnuska family. He is also by far the most shy and reserved wolfdog at the Sanctuary, due to many years of neglect on a property with 200 other dogs. Horton came to the Sanctuary in January 2015 as part of the Milk River Seizure carried out by the Alberta Society for the Prevention of Cruelty to Animals. Though he doesn't always let it show, he has a goofy and sweet personality, and adores his pack mate Kasha. He continues to make progress in how he relates to humans and is becoming a happy and healthy wolfdog!

Beard grooming with Horton

Start with a snow lather

Gently exfoliate with a natural bark rub

use an organic stump for chin whiskers

Complete the rugged look with a dusting of snow.

Kasha (upper-mid content)

Kasha is a real beauty who loves showing her long legs off to visitors! She is very curious but can be a bit reserved at times. Sometimes she does spook easily, but she very much enjoys some neck and ear scratches too. She came to Yamnuska from Oklahoma shortly after she was born in 2014, because her owners could no longer care for her.

Kasha:
YAMNUŠKA'S
TOP MODEL
Stand
MODELING!
Lie
Look

Temple Pack

Kaida & TK

Lazy day...
Get up, we have a photo shoot.
How about we wrestle instead?
Certainly!

Kaida (high content)

Kaida loves jumping into the water tanks to cool off on hot summer days! She's very well adjusted and enjoys socializing with visitors. She arrived at the Sanctuary as a puppy shortly after being born in Saskatchewan in the spring of 2014, and was raised by none other than the Yamnuska Pack! She went on to help raise the wolfdogs of the Engadine Pack, and her current pack mate TK. She has become a very tough girl and does a great job keeping mischief to a minimum!

Gardening with Kaida
A Weed!
I don't actually know what this is.
But I ate it.

TK (high content)

TK has one of the goofiest and happy-go-lucky personalities of all the wolfdogs at Yamnuska. He's also well known for not keeping still for very long — it can be challenging to get non-blurry photos of him unless he's asleep! He's very affectionate and loves to wrestle with his pack mate Kaida, but can be very particular about which people he's comfortable with. He came to the Sanctuary in November 2017 as an owner-surrender.

Did I sleep through the whole thing?
Oh well.

Engadine Pack

Aspen, Grizz & Quinn

(siblings!)

Aspen we need to wash for the photos!
Bath?
okay.
She got to you too?

Aspen (high content)

Compared to his siblings Grizz and Quinn, Aspen is the most shy and sensitive member of the Engadine pack — but also the most affectionate by far! While being a bit more timid with new people, once trust is gained, he becomes a big-time cuddler. After being born in May 2016 in Idaho, Aspen arrived at the Sanctuary in the summer of 2016.

wait. I smell...
Food!
STEALTH MODE!
Didn't even see me coming!
NOM NOM NOM

Grizz (high content)

Grizz knows that you know he's handsome, and is often seen striking a pose for the cameras. His unique blonde coat is the result of being a cross with both grey and arctic wolf. He has a bold personality and can be a bit of a troublemaker which — unsurprisingly — doesn't stop staff and visitors from loving him. Born in May 2016, Grizz arrived at the Sanctuary in the summer of 2016 with his two littermates, Quinn and Aspen, from an organization in Idaho.

The visitors definitely have food...
CHARM MODE!
Well Hello...
Why thank you!
NOM NOM NOM

Quinn (high content)

Quinn is incredibly confident and cuddly! She arrived at the Sanctuary in the summer of 2016 with her two brothers, Grizz and Aspen, and she's clearly the most dominant and fearless of the trio, regularly bossing her bigger brothers around! Don't let her bossy persona fool you, though — watch for the frequent play-breaks when she is cuddled up to one or both of her brothers! Quinn was born in May 2016 and came to Yamnuska from an organization in Idaho.

This belong
to anyone?
Anyone?
Going
once...
Going twice...
BOSS
MODE!

zzzzzZzzzz...

Nap Mode.

Galatea Pack

Freya & Odin

Come on, why so camera shy?
I HATE the way I look in photos.
Just do dignified wolf poses, like this. Come on, try one!
How's this?
Okay. Stop.

Freya (high content)

If you spot Freya, or are even lucky enough to get a photo of her, you'll notice that she's quite the supermodel! She has stunningly good looks and can definitely strike a pose. She's quite shy and timid of humans, but can be very curious about staff and visitors alike — watch out for her following you from a distance, hidden behind the trees! Freya loves her pack mate, Odin — they both moved to the Sanctuary in November 2017 from an organization in Smithers, British Columbia.

Odin (mid content)

Though Odin is quite shy of humans, he can be a huge goofball once you get to know him! He might even be the second biggest goofball in the Yamnuska wolfdog family — just guess who's first! He's also uniquely handsome thanks to the beautiful red and brown tones in his coat. Odin came to the Sanctuary in November 2017 with his pack mate, Freya.

Supper Time?

Hungry?

Nah,
I ate
already.

Without
me?

Alright, I'll
get myself
something...

NOM
NOM
NOM

Grotto Pack

Enzo & Ruby

Hey we doing the book photo?
Excuse me? What's that?
HEY.
Look serious!
Right. Serious.

Enzo

(upper-mid content)

Enzo is known for his dramatic facial expressions and incredibly long tail! He's a bit reserved, but can also be very sweet. He may appear to be a bit of a grump around people sometimes, but he's very kind to his fellow pack mate. Enzo was surrendered by his owner in November 2017.

You stay put...
I'll find a snack...
Hmm...
Salad
with Enzo

Ruby (mid content)

Ruby loves other canines almost as much as she loves being the boss! She enjoys playing with her pack mate but feels best calling the shots. Ruby came to Yamnuska in October 2017 as an owner-surrender after being purchased from a backyard breeder, and is quite shy of people. To get to Yamnuska, she came thousands of kilometers across the continent — she's originally from Newfoundland!

Yoga with Ruby
Your turn!

Norquay Pack

Kiba & Shadow

Kiba (low content)

Being at Yamnuska has been a real blessing for Kiba; she's becoming more comfortable with people and her goofy personality is beginning to show! Her unique look comes from the fact that she's mixed with Irish Wolfhound. Kiba came to the Sanctuary as one of 200 dogs in the Milk River Seizure that occurred in January 2015. Due to years of neglect, she is the most shy of all the wolfdogs at the Sanctuary.

Shadow (low content)

Shadow is quite reserved due to many years of neglect, but has made good progress towards being more comfortable with people. He came to the Sanctuary in January 2015 as one of the 200 dogs in the Milk River Seizure.

where are they hiding?

Kiba and Shadow live in an enclosure that's away from the Sanctuary trails. They're not quite ready to meet you... yet!

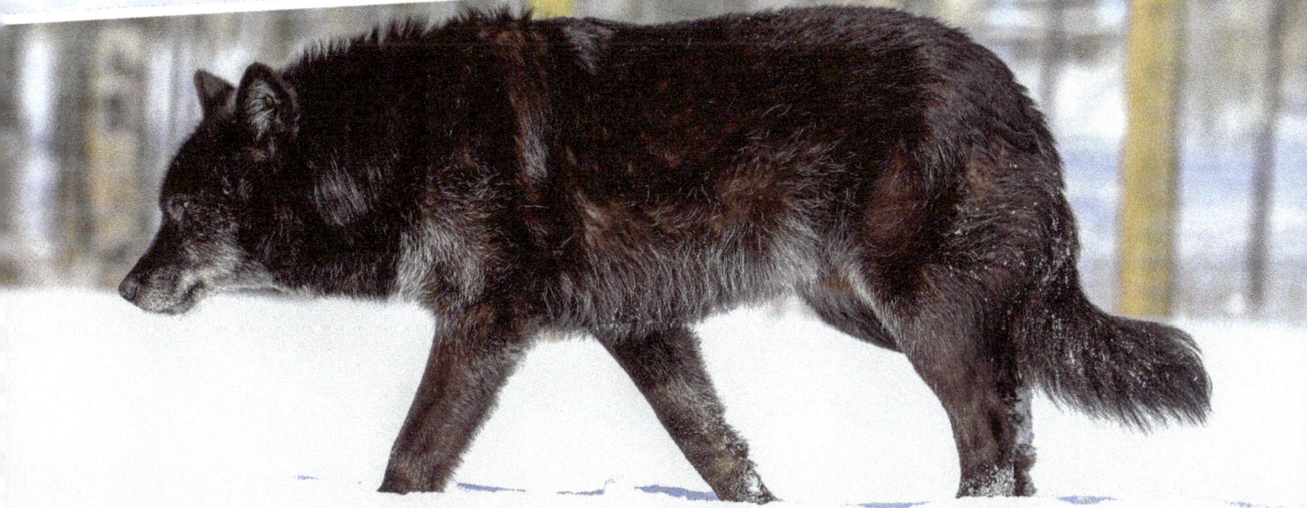

Pocaterra Pack

Lichen
& Mawko
(lovebirds)

Lichen (high content)

Lichen has a girlfriend! He adores his pack mate and love, Mawko, who helps him come out of his shell, bit by bit. Lichen came to the Sanctuary from a neglectful and abusive environment. Though he's not comfortable with direct human contact, he doesn't mind being viewed and photographed by visitors, and can also be quite curious.

Mawko (low content)

Mawko loves every opportunity she gets to interact with just about anyone! She is a very sweet girl who loves belly rubs. Being an exceptionally friendly wolfdog, she's taken on the important role of ambassador wolfdog at the Yamnuska Wolfdog Sanctuary. Mawko came to the Sanctuary when she found herself in a bit of a sticky situation after being unfairly deemed "aggressive" but she truly excels in her new environment and role.

I must receive today's human delegation!
Hmph.
Meet Ambassador Mawko
Delighted to meet you!
As is your custom, I offer my paw.
As is my custom, I stick out my tongue.
Yes, please continue petting me.

Later...
I'm back. Lots of humans today!
Sounds... exhausting...
They're nice. You'll see. Just have a nap.
They're still staring at us.
Hm. Okay. Love you.
You too.

yamnuskawolfdogsanctuary.com
@yamnuskawdsanct +1-587-890-WOLF (9653)

VISIT THE SANCTUARY

Located at 263156 Range Road 53, on the 1A highway, 60 minutes east of Banff National Park, Canada.

Open daily from Thursday to Monday, with full programming available most days.

Interactive Tours with the Yamnuska and Cascade Packs require bookings in advance. **Intro Tours** with the Engadine Pack do not require a reservation unless your group is more than 10 people. **Sanctuary Walks** do not require a reservation.

SUPPORT THE SANCTUARY

A portion of the proceeds from this book are being donated to support the Yamnuska Wolfdog Sanctuary, which depends heavily on the generosity of donors to help fund its important work.

Every donation helps feed, care for, transport, or rehome an adoptable wolfdog — or gives a high-content wolfdog a permanent home at the Sanctuary. Monetary donations are gratefully accepted, but select material donations are as well.

For details on how you can further support the Yamnuska Wolfdog Sanctuary, visit:

yamnuskawolfdogsanctuary.com/donate